Spanish First Names

Edited by
FRED JAMES HILL

HIPPOCRENE BOOKS
NEW YORK

Typeset & designed by Fred Hill & Nick Awde/Desert♥Hearts

ISBN 0-7818-0799-9

For information, address:
HIPPOCRENE BOOKS, INC.
171 Madison Avenue
New York, NY 10016

Printed in the United States of America.

Shortest Spanish name:

O

*From Maria de la O,
a name associated with
the Virgin Mary*

— ❦ —

Longest Spanish name:

Deoscopidesempérides

*A name of Latin origin meaning
'one who rests in the eternal
contemplation of God'*

Contents

Girls' Names

A

Aarona
Feminine form of **Aarón**
Hebrew — *haron* meaning 'high mountain'
Aaron was the brother of Moses

— ❧ —

Abigail
Hebrew — *avigayil* meaning 'father of joy'

— ❧ —

Adela
Germanic — *athal* meaning 'noble'
Alternative form: **Adelina**
Familiar forms: Ade, Dela, **Ela**

— ❧ —

Adelaida
Germanic — *athal* (noble) + *haidu* (type)

— ❧ —

Adelina
Form of **Adela**
Familiar form: **Lina**

— ❧ —

Adina
Hebrew — *adin* meaning 'slender'

— ❧ —

Adoración
Spanish — *adoración* meaning 'adoration'

— ❧ —

Adriana
Feminine form of **Adrián**
Latin — *Adrianus* meaning 'a man from the city of Adria'

— ❧ —

Ágata
Greek — *agathos* meaning 'kind'
Alternative form: **Águeda**

— ❧ —

Agnecita
Familiar form of **Inés**

— ❧ —

Águeda
Form of **Ágata**

— ❧ —

Agustina
Feminine form of **Agustín**
Latin — *augustus* meaning 'venerable, majestic,' a title originally
given to Roman emperors
Familiar form: **Tina**

— ❦ —

Ainoa
Basque — of obscure origin

— ❦ —

Aintzane
A name of Basque origin meaning 'glory'

— ❦ —

Aixa
Arabic — *aish* meaning 'alive, living well'
Aisha was the prophet Muhammad's favorite wife

— ❦ —

Alba
Latin — *alba* meaning 'white'

— ❦ —

Alegra
Latin — *allegra* meaning 'cheerful'
Alternative form: **Alegranza**

— ❦ —

Alegranza
Form of **Alegra**

— ❦ —

Alegría
Spanish — *alegría* meaning 'happiness, joy'

Alejandra
Feminine form of **Alejandro**
Greek — *alexein* (to protect, defend) + *andros* (man)
Familiar form: **Sandra**

Alicia
Germanic — *athal* (noble) + *heidu* (type)
Familiar forms: Ali, **Licia**

Alma
Spanish — *alma* meaning 'soul'

Almudena
Arabic — *al-mudeina* meaning 'small city'
A name associated with the Virgin Mary

Alvera
Feminine form of **Álvaro**
Old English — *ælf* (elf, supernatural being) + *here* (army)

Amalia
Greek — *amalos* meaning 'tender'
Familiar forms: **Amy, Lía**

— 🐝 —

Amanda
Latin — *amandus* meaning 'worthy of love'

— 🐝 —

Amaya
Basque — of obscure origin

— 🐝 —

Amelia
Germanic — *amal* meaning 'work'

— 🐝 —

Amira
Arabic — *amira* meaning 'princess'

— 🐝 —

Amparo
Spanish — *amparo* meaning 'refuge, protection'
A name associated with the Virgin Mary

— 🐝 —

Amy
Familiar form of **Amalia**

— 🐝 —

Ana
Hebrew — *hannah* meaning 'graceful'
Ana Figuero (1908-1970), Chilean feminist — the first woman
to head a UN Committee of the General Assembly (1951)
and the first woman on the Security Committee (1952)
Familiar forms: Any, **Nana**

— ❦ —

Anabel
Scottish — from *Annabel* a name of obscure origin

— ❦ —

Anastasia
Feminine form of **Anastasio**
Greek — *anastasis* meaning 'resurrection'

— ❦ —

Andrea
Feminine form of **Andrés**
Greek — *andreios* meaning 'manly'

— ❦ —

Ángela
Feminine form of **Ángel**
Greek — *angelos* meaning 'messenger'
Alternative form: **Ángeles**
Familiar forms: Ange, **Nana**

— ❦ —

Ángeles
Form of **Ángela**

— ❦ —

Angustias
Spanish — *angustia* meaning 'anguish'
A name associated with the Virgin Mary
— ❦ —

Antonia
Feminine form of **Antonio**
From *Antonius*, an old Roman family name of uncertain origin,
possibly from the Latin *antonius* meaning 'inestimable'
or the Greek *anthos* meaning 'flower'
Antonia Mercé (1890-1936), Argentinian-born Spanish dancer
Familiar forms: **Tonia, Toñeta, Toñy**
— ❦ —

Anunciación
Spanish — *anunciación* meaning 'announcement,'
referring to the Annunciation when Gabriel announced the future
birth of Jesus to Mary
— ❦ —

Apolonia
Feminine form of **Apolonio**
Greek — after *Apollo*, the Greek sun god
— ❦ —

Aquilina
Feminine form of **Aquilino**
Latin — *aquila* meaning 'eagle'
— ❦ —

Arabela
Of Scottish origin, possibly a form of **Annabel** from the Latin
amabilis meaning 'loveable' or from the Latin *orabilis* meaning
'yielding to prayer'
— ❦ —

Araceli
Latin — *ara* (altar) + *coeli* (of the sky)
Familiar form: **Celi**

— ❧ —

Arantxa
Form of **Aránzazu**
Arantxa Sánchez-Vicario (born 1971), Spanish tennis player

— ❧ —

Aránzazu
Basque — *Aránzazu* originally meaning 'hawthorn'
Alternative form: **Arantxa**

— ❧ —

Ariadna
Greek — *ari-adnos* meaning 'very holy'

— ❧ —

Arrene
A name of Basque origin meaning 'prayer'

— ❧ —

Artemisa
Greek — after *Artemis*, the Greek goddess of the moon

— ❧ —

Astrid
Germanic — *ansi* (god) + *drudi* (strength)

— ❧ —

Asunción
Spanish — *asunción* meaning 'assumption,'
referring to the Assumption of the Virgin Mary

— ❧ —

Aurelia
Latin — *aureus* meaning 'golden'

— ❧ —

Aurora
Latin — after *Aurora*, the Roman goddess of the dawn,
from *aurora* meaning 'dawn'

— ❧ —

Azucena
Spanish — *azucena* meaning '(white) lily,'
a Christian symbol of purity

— ❧ —

ℬ

Bárbara
Greek — *barbaros* meaning 'foreign, strange'

— ❦ —

Beatriz
Latin — *beatrix* meaning 'bearer of happiness'
Beatriz Galindo (1474-1534), Spanish humanist scholar
and professor of philosophy, rhetoric and medicine,
known as 'La Latina'
Familiar forms: Bea, Beti

— ❦ —

Begoña
Basque — *beg-oin-a* meaning 'the place of the dominant hill'
the name refers to a hill overlooking the city of Bilbao
in the Basque province of Vizcaya in Spain, where
there is a shrine to the **Virgin of Begoña,**
the patron of the region
Begoña is not related to **Begonia**, which is derived from
the flower of the same name

— ❦ —

Begonia
Spanish — *begonia* meaning 'begonia'

— ❦ —

Belén
After the town *Bethlehem*, from the Hebrew *bet-leem* meaning
'house of bread'
Familiar form: Bel

— ❧ —

Belinda
Germanic — of obscure origin

— ❧ —

Berenice
Greek — *pherenice* meaning 'bringer of victory'

— ❧ —

Berta
Germanic — *beraht* meaning 'bright, illustrious'

— ❧ —

Besi
Familiar form of **Elisabet**

— ❧ —

Betsabé
Hebrew — after *Bathsheba*, the beautiful wife of Uriah
in the Old Testament

— ❧ —

Blanca
Germanic — *blank* meaning 'white (pure)'
Blanca also means 'white' in Spanish
Familiar form: Blanqui

— ❧ —

Brenda
Possibly from the Norse *brandr* meaning 'sword'

— —

Brígida
After *Brigit*, the Celtic goddess of poetry

— —

C

Camelia
Latin — from *Camillus*, an old Roman family name of
obscure origin
Alternative form: **Camila**
Familiar forms: Melia, Mila

— ❦ —

Camila
Form of **Camelia**

— ❦ —

Candelaria
Spanish — *candelaria* meaning 'Candlemas'
A name associated with the Virgin Mary
Familiar form: Candi

— ❦ —

Caridad
Spanish — *caridad* meaning 'charity'

— ❦ —

Carina
Latin — *cara* meaning 'dear'

— ❦ —

Carlota
Feminine form of **Carlos**
Germanic — *karl* meaning 'adult male, man'

— ❦ —

Carmen
Hebrew — a name originating from Mount Carmel
in the Holy Land which later gave its name
to the Carmelite order of nuns
The Virgin Mary of Carmel is the patron of sailors and
one of the most venerated in Spain
Carmen also means 'song' or 'poem' in Spanish
Carmen Amaya (1913-1963), Spanish gypsy dancer
Carmen Maura (born 1945), Spanish actress

— 🐝 —

Carolina
Feminine form of **Carlos**
Germanic — *karl* meaning 'adult male, man'

— 🐝 —

Casandra
After *Cassandra*, the Greek princess of Troy who was able to foretell
future events but was never believed

— 🐝 —

Catalina
Greek — *katharos* meaning 'pure'
Catherine is the English form

— 🐝 —

Cecilia
Latin — from *Caecilius*, an old Roman family name originally from
the Latin *coecus* meaning 'blind'
Familiar form: Ceci

— 🐝 —

Celena

Possibly after *Selene*, the Greek goddess of the moon
or from the Latin *caelum* meaning 'heaven'

Celeste

Feminine form of **Celestino**
Latin — *caelestis* meaning 'heavenly'
Alternative form: **Celestina**

Celestina

Form of **Celeste**

Celi

Familiar form of **Araceli**

Celia

Latin — from *Caelius*, an old Roman family name of
obscure origin
Celia Cruz (born 1920), Cuban salsa singer

Cintia

Greek — from *kynthos*, the name of the mountain which was a
favorite place of *Artemis*, the Greek goddess of the moon
Kynthia became another name by which the goddess was known
Cynthia is the English form

Clara
Latin — *clarus* meaning 'clear'

— ❦ —

Clotilde
Germanic — *hlod* (glorious) + *hild* (battle)

— ❦ —

Concepción
Spanish — *concepción* meaning 'conception,'
referring to the Immaculate Conception of the Virgin Mary
Concepción Arenal (1820-1893), highly respected and influential
prize-winning Spanish social scientist, journalist and philanthropist
Familiar forms: **Concha**, Conchi, **Conchita**

— ❦ —

Concha/Conchita
Familiar forms of **Concepción**
Conchita Martínez (born 1972), Spanish tennis player

— ❦ —

Conseja
Spanish — *consejo* meaning 'advice, counsel'
A name associated with the Virgin Mary

— ❦ —

Consuelo
Spanish — *consuelo* meaning 'comfort, solace'
A name associated with the Virgin Mary
Familiar form: Lito

— ❦ —

Corazón
Spanish — *corazón* meaning 'heart'

— ❦ —

Cristina
Feminine form of **Cristián**
Latin — *christianus* meaning 'follower of Christ'
Familiar forms: Cris, **Nina**

— ❦ —

Cruz
Spanish — *cruz* meaning 'cross'

— ❦ —

$\mathcal{D}$

Daniela
Feminine form of **Daniel**
Hebrew — *daniel* meaning 'God is my judge'

Débora
Hebrew — *deborah* meaning 'bee'

Dela
Familiar form of **Adela**

Delia
Greek — *delos*, the legendary birthplace of *Artemis*, the Greek
goddess of the moon

Diana
Latin — after *Diana*, the Roman goddess of the moon and hunting

Dina
Hebrew — *dinah* meaning 'judged'

Dolores
Spanish — *dolor* meaning 'pain'
A name associated with the Virgin Mary
Dolores del Rio (1905-1983), Mexican actress
Familiar forms: **Lola**, Loles, Loli, **Lolita**

— ❧ —

Dorotea
Greek — *doron* (present) + *theos* (god)

— ❧ —

Dulce
Spanish — *dulce* meaning 'sweet'

— ❧ —

E

Ederne
A name of Basque origin meaning 'beautiful'

— ❧ —

Edita
Germanic — *ead* (riches) + *gyth* (struggle)

— ❧ —

Ela
Familiar form of **Adela**

— ❧ —

Elena
Greek — after *Helen of Troy*, the beautiful Greek queen, from
helenos meaning 'the bright, shining one'
Alternative forms: **Eleonor, Helena, Leonor**
Familiar forms: Ena, **Lena**

— ❧ —

Eleonor
Form of **Elena**

— ❧ —

Elisa
Form of **Elisabet**
Familiar forms: Eli, **Isa**

— ❧ —

Elisabet
Hebrew — *elisheba* meaning 'oath of God'
Alternative forms: **Elisa, Isabel, Isabella, Isabelina**
Familiar forms: Bes, **Besi**, Eli, **Licha**

— ❦ —

Eloísa
French — after *Heloise* (a name of obscure origin),
the lover of Abelard, whose famous love affair in the
12th century ended in tragedy

— ❦ —

Elvira
Germanic — possibly from *athal* (noble) + *wira* (guardian)
Familiar form: Elvi

— ❦ —

Emilia
Feminine form of **Emilio**
Latin — from *Aemilius* an old Roman family name meaning 'eager'
Emilia Pardon Bazán (1851-1921), Spanish novelist, feminist
and influential critic
Familiar forms: Emi, Mili

— ❦ —

Emma
German — *ermin* meaning 'universal'

— ❦ —

Encarnación
Spanish — *encarnación* meaning 'incarnation,'
referring to the act of God taking on the human form of Jesus
Basque form: **Maite**
Familiar forms: Encarna, Encarni, **Nita**

— ❦ —

Engracia
Latin — *gratia* meaning 'grace'
— 🐝 —

Enriqua
Feminine form of **Enrique**
Germanic — *haimi* (house) + *richi* (ruler)
Alternative form: **Enriqeta**
— 🐝 —

Enriqueta
Form of **Enriqua**
— 🐝 —

Esmeralda
Spanish — *esmeralda* meaning 'emerald'
— 🐝 —

Esperanza
Spanish — *esperanza* meaning 'hope'
Familiar forms: Espe, **Zita**
— 🐝 —

Estefanía
Feminine form of **Esteban**
Greek — *stephanos* meaning 'crown'
— 🐝 —

Estela
Latin — *stella* meaning 'star'
— 🐝 —

Ester
Possibly a Persian rendering of a Hebrew word
meaning 'myrtle'

— ❦ —

Estíbaliz
A name of Basque origin meaning 'sweet'

— ❦ —

Estrella
Spanish — *estrella* meaning 'star'

— ❦ —

Eufemia
Greek — *eu* (good) + *pheme* (speech)

— ❦ —

Eugenia
Feminine form of **Eugenio**
Greek — *eugenes* meaning 'well-born, noble'
Familiar form: Eny

— ❦ —

Eulalia
Greek — *eulalia* meaning 'eloquent'

— ❦ —

Eunice
Greek — *eu* (good) + *nike* (victory)

— ❦ —

Eva

Hebrew — after *hawwa* meaning 'life,' implying 'mother of all life'
Eva Perón (1919-1952), Argentinian political figure
popularly known as '**Evita**'
Familiar forms: **Evita**, Evy
Eve is the English form

— ❦ —

Evangelina

Greek — *euangelion* meaning 'good news'

— ❦ —

Evita

Familiar form of **Eva**

— ❦ —

Fabiola
Latin — from *Fabius*, an old Roman family name taken from the
Latin *faba* meaning 'broad bean'

— ❧ —

Fátima
Arabic — *fatim* meaning 'weaned'

— ❧ —

Febe
Greek — after *Phoibe* (Phoebe), the Greek goddess of the moon,
from *phoibos* meaning 'radiant'

— ❧ —

Federica
Feminine form of **Federico**
Germanic — *frithu* (peace) + *rik* (ruler)

— ❧ —

Felicidad
Spanish — *felicidad* meaning 'happiness'

— ❧ —

Filomena
Greek — *philomenes* meaning 'loving strength'

— ❧ —

Flor
Spanish — *flor* meaning 'flower'

— 🐝 —

Flora
After the Roman goddess of flowers, from the Latin *flos* (flower)

— 🐝 —

Florencia
Latin — *florens* meaning 'blooming'

— 🐝 —

Francisca
Feminine form of **Francisco**
Italian — *Francesco* meaning 'French'
Familiar form: **Paquita**

— 🐝 —

G

Gabriela
Feminine form of **Gabriel**
Hebrew — *gabhriel* meaning 'strong man of God'
Gabriella Mistral (1889-1957), Nobel Prize-winning Chilean poet,
novelist and diplomat
Gabriela Sabatini (born 1970), Argentinian tennis player
Familiar form: Gaby

— ❦ —

Garbiñe
A name of Basque origin meaning 'immaculate'

— ❦ —

Gema
Spanish — *gema* meaning 'gem, precious stone'

— ❦ —

Genoveva
Germanic — possibly from *geno* (tribe, people) + *wifa* (woman)

— ❦ —

Gisela
Germanic — *gisil* meaning 'arrow'

— ❦ —

Gloria
Latin — *gloria* meaning 'glory, praise'

— ❦ —

Gracia
Latin — *gratia* meaning 'grace'
Alternative form: **Graciela**

— ❧ —

Graciela
Form of **Gracia**

— ❧ —

Griselda
Germanic — of obscure origin

— ❧ —

Guadalupe
Arabic — *wadi-lupi* meaning 'river of the wolves'
Lupe Velez (1908-1944), Mexican actress
Familiar form: **Lupe**

— ❧ —

H

Helena
Form of **Elena**

— ❧ —

Hilda
Germanic — *hild* meaning 'battle'

— ❧ —

I

Iciar
A name of Basque origin meaning 'high point facing the sea'

— ❦ —

Imelda
Germanic — *ermen* (universal) + *hild* (battle)

— ❦ —

Inés
Greek — *agne* meaning 'pure'
Familiar forms: **Agnecita, Sita**
Agnes is the English form

— ❦ —

Ingrid
After *Ing*, the Norse goddess of fertility

— ❦ —

Inmaculada
Latin — *in-macula* meaning 'without stain'
Familiar form: **Inma**

— ❦ —

Irene
Greek — *eirene* meaning 'peace'

— ❦ —

Irma
Germanic — *ermen* meaning 'universal, complete'

— ❧ —

Isa
Familiar form of **Elisa**

— ❧ —

Isabel
Form of **Elisabet**
Isabel Allende (born 1942), Chilean writer

— ❧ —

Isabelina
Form of **Elisabet**

— ❧ —

Isabella
Form of **Elisabet**
Isabella I (1451-1504), Queen of Castile (1447-1504) also known
as **Isabella the Catholic**, married King **Ferdinand** of Aragon and
created a union of the two most powerful Iberian kingdoms
leading to the creation of the Spanish nation-state
Together they were responsible for sending
Christopher Columbus to America in 1492

— ❧ —

Isidora
Feminine form of **Isidoro**
Greek — *Isis* (the Greek goddess of fertility) + *doron* (gift)

— ❧ —

J

Javiera
Feminine form of **Javier**
Basque — *etxe-berri* meaning 'new house'

— ❦ —

Jazmín
Arabic — *yasamin* meaning 'jasmine'
Alternative form: **Yasmina**

— ❦ —

Jessica
Of obscure origin

— ❦ —

Joaquina
Feminine form of **Joaquín**
Hebrew — *yehoyakim* meaning 'God constructs'
Familiar form: **Quina**

— ❦ —

Josefa
Feminine form of **José**
Hebrew — *yosef* meaning 'He shall add (another son)'
Familiar forms: Sefa, Sefita, Pepa, Pepina

— ❦ —

Juana

Feminine form of **Juan**

Hebrew — *Yohanan* meaning 'God has been gracious'

Juana de Ibarbourou (1895-1979), Uruguayan poet and author
who was so popular that she was given the title
'Juana de America'

Familiar form: **Nita**

— ❧ —

Judit

Hebrew — *jehudit* meaning 'a Jewish woman'

— ❧ —

Julia

Feminine form of **Julio**

Latin — from *Julius*, an old Roman family name of obscure origin

Alternative forms: **Julieta**

Familiar forms: **Lía, Liana,** Chula

— ❧ —

Julieta

Form of **Julia**

— ❧ —

L

Laura
Latin — *laurus* meaning 'laurel'

— ❦ —

Lavinia
Latin — After *Lavinia* in Roman mythology, the daughter of King
Latinus and wife of Aeneas who was considered the
mother of the Roman people

— ❦ —

Ledia
Greek — of obscure origin

— ❦ —

Leila
Arabic — *laïla* meaning 'night,' perhaps referring to dark hair

— ❦ —

Lena
Familiar form of **Elena**

— ❦ —

Leonor
Form of **Elena**

— ❦ —

Leticia
Latin — *laetitia* meaning 'happiness'

— ❧ —

Lía
Familiar form of **Amalia** and **Julia**

— ❧ —

Liana
Familiar form of **Julia**

— ❧ —

Libertad
Spanish — *libertad* meaning 'liberty, freedom'

— ❧ —

Libia
Greek — *Libia* meaning 'from the North African country of Libya'

— ❧ —

Licha
Familiar form of **Elisabet**

— ❧ —

Licia
Familiar form of **Alicia**

— ❧ —

Lidia
Greek — *Lydia* meaning 'woman from Lydia,' the 6th century
kingdom which covered most of Asia Minor

— ❧ —

Lilia
Latin — *lilium* meaning 'lily,' a Christian symbol of purity
— ❦ —

Lina
Familiar form of **Adelina**
— ❦ —

Linda
Spanish — *linda* meaning 'beautiful'
— ❦ —

Liria
Spanish — feminine form of the word *lirio* meaning 'iris'
— ❦ —

Lola/Lolita
Familiar forms of **Dolores**
Lola Beltrán (died 1996), Mexican singer, known as the 'Queen of Ranchera'
— ❦ —

Lorena
From the French *Lorraine*, a province of France, meaning a person from this region
— ❦ —

Lourdes
Basque — *lorde* meaning 'steep slope' and the name of the pilgrim town Lourdes, in southern France, where the Virgin Mary appeared to Bernadette
— ❦ —

Lucía
Latin — *lux* meaning 'light'

— ❧ —

Luisa
Feminine form of **Luis**
Germanic — *hluda* (famous) + *wiga* (war)

— ❧ —

Lupe
Familiar form of **Guadalupe**

— ❧ —

Luz
Spanish — *luz* meaning 'light'
A name associated with the Virgin Mary

— ❧ —

M

Mafalda
Germanic — *maht* (might) + *hild* (battle)

— ❧ —

Magdalena
After Mary of Magdala (a town on Lake Galilee)
Familiar form: Magda

— ❧ —

Maite
Basque form of **Encarnación**

— ❧ —

Manuela
Feminine form of **Manuel**
Hebrew — *immanuel* meaning 'God is with us'
Familiar form: Manolita

— ❧ —

Maravillas
Spanish — *maravilla* meaning 'wonder, marvel'

— ❧ —

Marcela
Form of **Marcia**

— ❧ —

Marcia
Feminine form of **Marco**
Latin — from *Marcus*, an old Roman family name probably derived
from *Mars*, the Roman god of war
Alternative form: **Marcela**
— ❦ —

Margarita
Greek — *margaron* meaning 'pearl'
Familiar form: **Rita**
— ❦ —

María
Hebrew — *Miryam* of uncertain meaning
María Casares (Quiroga) (born 1922), Spanish-born theater and
film actress, considered one of France's leading actresses
Familiar form: Marí
Basque form: **Miren**
Mary is the English form
— ❦ —

María Antonia
See **María** and **Antonia**
— ❦ —

María del Carmen
See **María** and **Carmen**
— ❦ —

María del Pilar
See **María** and **Pilar**
— ❦ —

Maribel
A combination of **María** and **Isabel**
— ❦ —

— ❦ —

Marina
Latin — *marinus* meaning 'sailor'

— ❦ —

Marisol
A combination of **María** and **Soledad**

— ❦ —

Marta
Aramaic — *marta* meaning 'lady'

— ❦ —

Matilde
Germanic — *maht* (mighty) + *hild* (battle)

— ❦ —

Maya
Latin — *maius* meaning '(the month of) *Maia*' or 'May'
Maia was a Roman goddess

— ❦ —

Mercedes
Spanish — *merced* meaning 'mercy'
Mercedes Sosa, Argentinian singer
Familiar forms: Meche, Mercé, Merche

— ❦ —

Milagros
Spanish — *milagro* meaning 'miracle'
A name associated with the Virgin Mary
Familiar form: Mili

— ❦ —

Miranda
Latin — *mirandus* meaning 'astonished, amazed'

— ❦ —

Miren
Basque form of **María**

— ❦ —

Mireya
Taken from the Provençal form of *Mary*

— ❦ —

Míriam
Hebrew — *miryam* of uncertain meaning

— ❦ —

Mona
Familiar form of **Ramona**

— ❦ —

Montserrat
Catalan — after the Virgin of Montserrat, Patron of Cataluña
From *mont-serrat* meaning 'jagged mountain'
Montserrat Caballé (born 1933), Spanish soprano
Familiar forms: Montse, Montsita

— ❦ —

N

Naila
Arabic — *nala* meaning 'to give'

— 🐝 —

Nana
Familiar form of **Ana**

— 🐝 —

Natalia
Latin — *nativitas* meaning 'birth, nativity'
Familiar forms: **Tali**, **Talia**

— 🐝 —

Natividad
Latin — *nativitas* meaning 'birth, nativity'

— 🐝 —

Nereida
Greek — *nereid* meaning 'sea nymph'

— 🐝 —

Nieves
Spanish — *nieve* meaning 'snow'
A name associated with the Virgin Mary

— 🐝 —

Nina
Familiar form of **Cristina**

— ❦ —

Nita
Familiar form of **Encarnación** and **Juana**

— ❦ —

Noemí
Hebrew — *no'omi* meaning 'my sweetness'

— ❦ —

Nuria
Basque — *n-uri-a* meaning 'place between hills' after the
Virgin of Nuria

— ❦

O

Obdulia
Feminine form of the Arabic first name *Abdullah*
Arabic — *abd* (servant) + *allah* (God) meaning 'God's servant'

— ❦ —

Octavia
Feminine form of **Octavio**
Latin — *octavus* meaning 'eighth'

— ❦ —

Odilia
Germanic — *od* meaning 'wealth, prosperity'

— ❦ —

Olga
Germanic — *heilag* meaning 'holy'
Taken directly from the Russian first name *Olga*

— ❦ —

Olivia
Latin — *oliva* meaning 'olive'

— ❦ —

Ondina
Spanish — *ondina* meaning 'little wave'

— ❦ —

P

Paciencia
Spanish — *paciencia* meaning 'patience'

— ❦ —

Paloma
Spanish — *paloma* meaning 'dove'

— ❦ —

Paquita
Familiar form of **Francisca**

— ❦ —

Patricia
Latin — *patricius* meaning 'noble'
Familiar form: Pati

— ❦ —

Paula
Feminine form of **Pablo**
Latin — *paulus* meaning 'small'
Alternative forms: **Paulina**

— ❦ —

Paulina
Form of **Paula**

— ❦ —

Paz
Spanish — *paz* meaning 'peace'
A name associated with the Virgin Mary
— ❧ —

Penélope
Greek — after *Penelope*, who in Greek legend was the faithful wife
of Odysseus who waited ten years for his return
— ❧ —

Petronila
Latin — from *Petronius*, an old Roman family name taken from the
Greek *petros* meaning 'rock, stone'
— ❧ —

Pilar
Spanish — *pilar* meaning 'pillar'
A name associated with the Virgin Mary
Familiar forms: Pili, Pilucha, Piluchi
— ❧ —

Priscila
Latin — diminutive of *prisca* meaning 'old, primitive'
— ❧ —

Prudencia
Latin — *prudens* meaning 'prudent'
— ❧ —

Purificación
Spanish — *purificación* meaning 'purification'
Familiar form: **Puri**
— ❧ —

2

Quina
Familiar form of **Joaquina**

R

Rafaela
Feminine form of **Rafael**
Hebrew — *rafael* meaning 'God has cured'
Familiar forms: Rafa, Rafita

— ❦ —

Ramona
Feminine form of **Ramón**
Germanic — *ragin* (wise) + *mund* (protection)
Familiar form: **Mona**

— ❦ —

Raquel
Hebrew — *rahel* meaning 'ewe'
Rachel is the English form

— ❦ —

Rebeca
Hebrew — after *Rebekah*, the beautiful wife of Isaac in the
Old Testament

— ❦ —

Regina
Latin — *regina* meaning 'queen'

— ❦ —

Remedios
Spanish — *remedio* meaning 'remedy'
A name associated with the Virgin Mary

— ❦ —

Reyes
Spanish — *rey* meaning 'king'
The name refers to the Three Kings in the Gospel

— ❦ —

Rita
Familiar form of **Margarita**

— ❦ —

Rocío
Spanish — *rocío* meaning 'dew'
A name associated with the Virgin Mary

— ❦ —

Rosa
Spanish — *rosa* meaning 'rose'

— ❦ —

Rosalía
Latin — *rosalia*, a Roman festival held in May in which roses were
thrown on tombs

— ❦ —

Rosalinda
From the Germanic *Roslindis*, a name of uncertain origin

— ❦ —

Rosamunda
Germanic — *hros* (horse) + *mund* (protection)

— ❦ —

Rosario
Spanish — *rosario* meaning 'rosary'
A name associated with the Virgin Mary
Familiar forms: Charito, Charo

— ❦ —

S

Sabina
Latin — *Sabina* meaning 'a Sabine woman' (a member of the
Sabines, an ancient tribe living in the region of Italy)

Sandra
Familiar form of **Alejandra**

Sara
Hebrew — *sarah* meaning 'princess'
Sarah was the wife of Abraham in the Old Testament
Sara de Ibañez (1909-1971), Uruguayan poet, writer of intense
mystical verse
Familiar forms: Sari, Sarita

Silvia
Latin — *silva* meaning 'forest'
Familiar form: Silvy

—

Sita
Familiar form of **Inés**

—

Sofía
Greek — *sophia* meaning 'wisdom'

— ❦ —

Soledad
Spanish — *soledad* meaning 'solitude, loneliness'
A name associated with the Virgin Mary
Soledad Acosta de Sampar (1833-1903), Colombian writer and
defender of women's rights

— ❦ —

Susana
Hebrew — *shoshan* meaning 'lily'

— ❦ —

T

Tali/Talia
Familiar forms of **Natalia**

— ❦ —

Teresa
Of obscure origin
The name Teresa has long been associated with Spain
Teresa was first recorded in the 5th century as the name of the wife
of St. Paulinus who lived in Spain
St. Teresa of Avila (1515-1582), a Spanish Carmelite mystic, who
was responsible for the enormous popularity of the name
throughout the Roman Catholic world
Familiar form: Tere

— ❦ —

Tina
Familiar form of **Agustina**

— ❦ —

Tonia
Familiar form of **Antonia**

— ❦ —

Toñy/Toñeta
Familiar forms of **Antonia**

— ❦ —

Trinidad
Spanish — *trinidad* meaning 'trinity,' referring to the Holy Trinity

—

U

Úrsula
Latin — diminutive form of *ursa* meaning 'little she-bear'

𝒱

Vanesa
From the English *Vanessa*, a name invented by the
18th century English writer Jonathan Swift (1667-1745), who
used the name in a poem to refer to Esther Vanhomrigh
who was in love with him

— 🐝 —

Verónica
Of obscure origin

Victoria
Latin — *victor* meaning 'victorious'
Victoria Ocampo (1890-1978), highly influential Argentinian
writer, literary editor and champion of women's rights
Victoria de los Angeles (born 1923), internationally acclaimed
Spanish soprano

— 🐝 —

Violeta
Latin — *viola* meaning 'violet'
Violeta Parra (1917-1967), Chilean singer, folklorist and
songwriter

Virginia
Latin — *virgo* meaning 'virgin'

Υ

Yasmina
Form of Jazmín

— ❦ —

Yolanda
Greek — *iolanthe* meaning 'violet'
Familiar form: Yoli

— ❦ —

Z

Zenaida
Greek — after *Zeneida*, the daughter of Zeus in Greek mythology

Zita
Familiar form of **Esperanza**

Zoé
Greek — *zoe* meaning 'life'

Boys' Names

Aarón
Hebrew — *haron* meaning 'high mountain'
— ❧ —

Abel
Hebrew — *hebhel* similar to Assyrian *ablu* meaning 'son'
— ❧ —

Abraham
Hebrew — *Abraham* meaning 'father of a multitude'
— ❧ —

Absalón
Hebrew — *absalom* meaning 'peace of the father'
— ❧ —

Abundio
Latin — *abundans* meaning 'abundant, plenty'
San Abundio was a Spanish saint who was martyred in Córdoba by the Muslims in 854
— ❧ —

Adalberto
Germanic — *athal* (noble) + *beraht* (bright)
— ❦ —

Adán
Hebrew — *adamah* meaning 'earth'
— ❦ —

Adolfo
Germanic — *athal* (noble) + *wulf* (wolf)
Familiar form: **Dolfo**
— ❦ —

Adrián
Latin — *Adrianus* meaning 'a man from the city of Adria'
— ❦ —

Agustín
Latin — *augustus* meaning 'venerable, majestic,'
a title originally given to Roman emperors
Alternative form: Augustino, **Augusto**
Familiar form: **Tino**
— ❦ —

Aitor
Basque — *aita* meaning 'father'
Aitor was the name given to the legendary founder of the
Basque people
— ❦ —

Aladino
Arabic — *ala* (greatness) + *al-din* (the religion) meaning
'the greatness of religion'
— ❦ —

Alán
Celtic — of uncertain origin
— ❦ —

Alarico
Germanic — *athal* (noble) + *rik* (king)
— ❦ —

Alberto
Germanic — *athal* (noble) + *beraht* (bright)
Familiar form: **Berto**
— ❦ —

Aldo
Germanic — *athal* meaning 'noble'
— ❦ —

Alejandro
Greek — *alexein* (to protect, defend) + *andros* (man)
Familiar forms: Alex, **Jandro**
— ❦ —

Alexis
Greek — *alexein* meaning 'to protect, defend'
— ❦ —

Alfonso
Germanic — *athal* (noble) + *funsa* (ready)
Thirteen Spanish kings bore the name, starting with
Alfonso I of Aragón and Navarre (1073-1134) and ending with
Alfonso XIII (1886-1941)
Saint Alfonso (died 1617), Jesuit and patron saint of Majorca and
Palma, two of the Spanish Balearic islands in the Mediterranean
Familiar forms: Al, Alf
— ❦ —

Alfredo

Old English — *ælf* (elf, supernatural being) + *ræd* (counsel)
The name implies 'wisdom' owing to the special powers of elves
Familiar form: Alfi

— ❦ —

Almanzor

Arabic — *al-mansur* meaning 'the one aided by God'
or 'the victorious one'

— ❦ —

Álvaro

Old English — *ælf* (elf, supernatural being) + *here* (army)
Saint Álvaro of Cordoba was a Spanish missionary during
the 15th century
Álvaro Obregón (1880-1928), Mexican revolutionary leader

— ❦ —

Amadeo

Latin — *ama* (love) + *deus* (God)

— ❦ —

Amado

Spanish — *amado* meaning 'beloved, dear'

— ❦ —

Amador

Spanish — *amador* meaning 'lover'

— ❦ —

Amai
Basque — of obscure origin

— ❧ —

Amancio
Latin — *amantius* meaning 'loving'

— ❧ —

Ambrosio
Greek — *ambrosius* meaning 'immortal'

— ❧ —

Anastasio
Greek — *anastasis* meaning 'resurrection'

— ❧ —

Andrés
Greek — *andreios* meaning 'manly'
Andrés Segovia (1893-1987), Spanish guitar virtuoso
Andy Garcia (born Andrés Arturo García-Menéndez, 1956),
Cuban-born American actor
Andrés Eloy Blanco (1896-1955), Venezuelan poet
Andrew is the English form

— ❧ —

Ángel
Greek — *angelos* meaning 'messenger'
Ángel is often combined with **Miguel** to give **Miguel Ángel**
Familiar forms: **Gelo**, **Gelito**

— ❧ —

Aniceto
Greek — *aniketos* meaning 'unconquerable'

Anselmo
Germanic — *ansi* (divinity) + *helm* (helmet, protection)
— ❦ —

Antón
Form of **Antonio**
— ❦ —

Antonio
From *Antonius*, an old Roman family name of uncertain origin,
possibly from the Latin *antonius* meaning 'inestimable'
or the Greek *anthos* meaning 'flower'
Antonio Banderas (born 1960), Spanish actor
Alternative form: **Antón**
Familiar form: **Tonio**

Apolonio
Greek — after *Apollo*, the Greek sun god
— ❦ —

Aquiles
Greek — after *Achilles*, the warrior in the Trojan War
— ❦ —

Aquilino
Latin — *aquila* meaning 'eagle'

Arístides
Greek — *aristos* meaning 'best'
— ❦ —

Armando
Germanic — *heri* (army) + *man* (man)
— ❦ —

Arnaldo
Germanic — *arn* (eagle) + *waldan* (strength)
— ❦ —

Arnulfo
Germanic — *arn* (eagle) + *wulf* (wolf)
— ❦ —

Arquímedes
Greek — *archi* (chief) + *medesthai* (to ponder)
— ❦ —

Arsenio
Greek — *arsen* meaning 'virile'
— ❦ —

Artemio
Greek — after *Artemis*, the Greek goddess of the moon
— ❦ —

Arturo
Possibly from the Celtic *artos* meaning 'bear'
Arturo de Cordova (1908-1973), Mexican actor
Familiar forms: **Ito, Turo**
Arthur is the English form
— ❦ —

Atanasio
Greek — *athanasia* meaning 'immortality'

— ❦ —

Augusto
Form of **Agustín**

— ❦ —

Aurelio
Latin — *auruius* meaning 'golden'

— ❦ —

B

Baldomero
Germanic — *wald* (ruler) + *mari* (famous)

— ❧ —

Balduino
Germanic — *bald* (bold, brave) + *wine* (friend)

— ❧ —

Baltasar
After *Belshazzar*, the name given to one of the Three Kings
in the Gospel, from the Syrian *bal-tas-assar* meaning
'Baal protect the king'

— ❧ —

Bartolomé
Hebrew — *bar-Tolomai* meaning 'son of Talmai'
Bartolomé de las Casas (1474-1566), 16th century Dominican friar
who was a defender of Indian rights and campaigned to have
slavery abolished in Spanish America

— ❧ —

Basilio
Greek — *basileois* meaning 'royal'

— ❧ —

Bautista
Latin — *baptista* meaning 'a person who baptises,'
after St. John the Baptist

— ❦ —

Beltrán
Germanic — *berht* (bright) + *hramn* (raven)
The name implies wisdom, as ravens symbolized
this quality in German mythology

— ❦ —

Benigno
Latin — *benignus* meaning 'kind'

— ❦ —

Benito
Latin — *benedictus* meaning 'blessed, holy'
Benito Juárez (1806-1872), Zapotec Indian lawyer who became the
first elected civilian president of Mexico (1861-1872)
Benito Pérez Galdós (1843-1920), one of the greatest
Spanish novelists
Familiar forms: Beni, **Nito**

— ❦ —

Benjamín
Hebrew — *ben* (son) + *yamin* (right hand) meaning
'son of my right hand'

— ❦ —

Berna
Familiar form of **Bernardo**

— ❦ —

Bernabé
Greek — *barnabus* meaning 'son of exhortation or consolation'

Bernardo
Germanic — *berin* (bear) + *hard* (strong)
Familiar forms: **Berna, Nardo**

Berto
Familiar form of **Alberto** and **Roberto**

Blas
Latin — *blaesus* meaning 'stuttering'

Borís
Slavic — *bor* meaning 'battle'

Borja
After *San Francisco de Borja*
The name (meaning 'hut' or 'cabin') comes from Aragón in the northeast of Spain and is now used as a first name

Bruno
Germanic — *brun* meaning 'brown'

— ❦ —

Buenaventura
Latin — *bona* (good) + *ventura* (fortune)

— 🐝 —

C

Calito
Familiar form of **Cristóbal**

Calixto
Greek — *kallos* meaning 'the most handsome'

Camilo
Latin — from *Camillus*, an old Roman family name of
obscure origin

Carlos
Germanic — *karl* meaning 'adult male, man'
Carlos Fuentes (born 1928), Mexican writer and author
Carlos Gardel (1890-1935), Argentinian tango singer
Carlos Saura (born 1932), Spanish director and screenwriter
Charles is the English form

Cayetano
Latin — *caietanus* meaning 'from the city of Gaeta,'
in southern Italy
Alternative form: **Cayo**

Cayo
Form of **Cayetano**
— ❧ —

Celestino
Latin — *caelestis* meaning 'heavenly'
— ❧ —

Celso
Latin — from *Celsus*, an old Roman family name meaning 'tall'
— ❧ —

Cirilo
Greek — *kyrios* meaning 'lord'
— ❧ —

Claudio
Latin — from *Claudius*, an old Roman family name derived from
claudus meaning 'lame'
— ❧ —

Clemente
Latin — *clemens* meaning 'merciful'
— ❧ —

Cornelio
Latin — *cornu* meaning 'horn'
— ❧ —

Cristián
Latin — *christianus* meaning 'follower of Christ'
— ❧ —

Cristo
Greek — *chriein* meaning 'to anoint'
— ❦ —

Cristóbal
Greek — *Kristos* (Christ) + *pherein* (to bear) meaning
'bearer of Christ'
Cristoforo Colombo (1451-1506), the Italian explorer who in the
service of Spain was the first modern European to discover
America, is known to the Spanish-speaking world as **Cristóbal
Colón** and to the English-speaking world as
Christopher Columbus
Familiar forms: **Calito**, Cris, **Cristo**, **Lito**
— ❦ —

Cruz
Spanish — *cruz* meaning 'cross'
— ❦ —

Cuauhtémoc
From *Cuahtémoc*, an old Aztec name meaning 'descending eagle'
— ❦ —

Cugat
A Catalan name of obscure Carthaginian origin
— ❦ —

D

Dado
Familiar form of **Eduardo**

— ❦ —

Damaso
Greek — possibly from *daman* meaning 'to tame'

— ❦ —

Damián
Greek — possibly from *daman* meaning 'to tame'
After the Greek *Damianos*, brother of *Kosmas*, both of whom were
martyred in the early 4th century

— ❦ —

Daniel
Hebrew — *daniel* meaning 'God is my judge'
Familiar form: Dani

— ❦ —

Darío
Persian — *darayaraus* meaning 'active'

— ❦ —

David
Hebrew — *david* meaning 'beloved'
David Alfaro Siquieros (1896-1974), Mexican artist and muralist

— ❦ —

Demetrio
Greek — *demetrios* meaning 'follower of Demeter,' the Greek
goddess of agriculture and fertility

— ❦ —

Deri
Familiar form of **Federico**

— ❦ —

Diego
Form of the Spanish name **Jaime** from the Hebrew *yaaqob*
meaning 'supplanter'
Diego Rivera (1886-1957), Mexican artist and muralist

— ❦ —

Dionisio
Greek — after *Dionysos*, the Greek god of wine

— ❦ —

Dolfo
Familiar form of **Adolfo**

— ❦ —

Domingo
Latin — *dominus* meaning 'lord'
Familiar form: **Mingo**

— ❦ —

Donato
Latin — *donatus* meaning 'given'

— ❦ —

ℰ

Edmundo
Old English — *eadig* (fortune, rich) + *mund* (guardian)

— ❧ —

Eduardo
Germanic — *eadig* (fortune, rich) + *weard* (guardian, protector)
Familiar forms: **Dado**, Duardo, **Lalo**

— ❧ —

Efraín
Hebrew — *ephrayim* meaning 'fruitful'

— ❧ —

Eladio
Greek — *helladios* meaning 'Greek'

— ❧ —

Elías
Hebrew — *eliyahu* meaning 'Jehova is God'

— ❧ —

Eliseo
Hebrew — *elisha* meaning 'God is salvation'

— ❧ —

Eloy
Latin — *eligius* meaning 'chosen'

— ❧ —

Emilio

Latin — from *Aemilius*, an old Roman family name meaning 'eager'
Emiliano Zapata (1879-1919), Mexican revolutionary leader
Alternative form: Emiliano

— ❦ —

Enrique

Germanic — *haimi* (house) + *richi* (ruler)
Enrique Granados (1867-1916), Spanish composer
Familiar form: **Quique**
Henry is the English form

— ❦ —

Epifanio

Greek — *epiphaneia* meaning 'manifestation'

— ❦ —

Erasmo

Greek — *eran* meaning 'love'

— ❦ —

Ernesto

Germanic — *eornust* meaning 'seriously determined'
Ernesto Zedillo (born 1951), President of Mexico
Ernesto 'Che' Guevara (1928-1967), Argentinian-born
Latin American revolutionary leader
Familiar form: **Nesti**

— ❦ —

Estanislao

Slavonic — *stan* (government) + *slav* (glory)

— ❦ —

Esteban
Greek — *stephanos* meaning 'crown'
Familiar forms: Steve, **Tebe**,
Stephen is the English form
— 🐝 —

Eugenio
Greek — *eugenes* meaning 'well-born, noble'
Familiar form: **Geni**
— 🐝 —

Eurico
Germanic — *ehre* (honor) + *rik* (king)
— 🐝 —

Eusebio
Greek — *eusebios* meaning 'pious'
— 🐝 —

Evaristo
Greek — *euarestos* meaning 'very pleasing'
— 🐝 —

Ezequiel
Hebrew — *yehezqel* meaning 'God strengthens'
— 🐝 —

Fabián

Latin — from *Fabius*, an old Roman family name derived from *faba*
meaning 'broad bean'
Alternative form: **Fabio**

— ❧ —

Fabio

Form of **Fabián**

— ❧ —

Fausto

Latin — *fauste* meaning 'lucky, fortunate'

— ❧ —

Federico

Germanic — *frithu* (peace) + *rik* (ruler)
Federico García Lorca (1899-1936), Spanish poet and playwright
Familiar forms: **Deri**, Fede

— ❧ —

Felipe

Greek — *philos* (loving) + *hippos* (horses)
Felipe González (born 1942), Prime Minister of Spain (1982-1996)
Prince Felipe (born 1968), youngest child of **Juan Carlos I**,
King of Spain
Phillip is the English form

— ❧ —

Félix
Latin — *felix* meaning 'happy'

— ✢ —

Ferdinando
Older form of **Fernando**
Ferdinando el Catolico (1452-1516), King of Aragón,
married **Isabella I**, Queen of Castile (1474-1504) and created a
union of the two most powerful Iberian kingdoms leading to the
creation of the Spanish nation-state —
together, they were responsible for sending Christopher Columbus
to America in 1492

— ✢ —

Fermín
Latin — *firmus* meaning 'firm'
San Fermín, a 14th century martyr, is the patron saint of the
Basque province of Navarra in the north of Spain —
the saint gives his name to the festival of
San Fermín in Pamplona
Familiar form: **Mini**

— ✢ —

Fernando
Germanic — possibly from *frad* (intelligent) + *nand* (brave)
Fernando Botero (born 1932), Colombian artist
Alternative form: **Hernán**
Familiar form: **Nando**

— ✢ —

Fidel
Latin — *fidelis* meaning 'faithful'
Fidel Castro (born 1927), President of Cuba
Familiar form: Fido

— ❧ —

Filemón
Greek — *philemon* meaning 'affectionate'

— ❧ —

Filiberto
Germanic — *fila* (much) + *beraht* (bright)

— ❧ —

Florencio
Latin — *florens* meaning 'blossoming, flourishing'

— ❧ —

Fortunato
Latin — *fortunatus* meaning 'fortunate, lucky'

— ❧ —

Fortunio
Latin — *fortuno* meaning 'fortune'

— ❧ —

Francisco
Italian — *francesco* meaning 'French'
Francisco José de Goya (1746-1828), Spanish painter and etcher
Francisco Pizarro (1476-1541), Spanish conquistador
Familiar forms: Frasquito, **Paco**, **Pancho**, **Paquirrín**

— ❧ —

Fulgencio
Latin — *fulgens* meaning 'shining'

— 🐝 —

G

Gabriel
Hebrew — *gabhriel* meaning 'strong man of God'
Gabriel García Márquez (born 1928), Colombian writer and
Nobel Prize winner (1982) whose novels include
One Hundred Years of Solitude (1967)
Familiar form: Gaby

— ❦ —

Gaspar
Persian — *genashber* after the name given to one of the
Three Kings in the Gospel

— ❦ —

Gelito
Familiar form of **Ángel**

— ❦ —

Gelo
Familiar form of **Ángel**

— ❦ —

Genaro
Latin — *Januarius* meaning 'the month of January'

— ❦ —

Geni
Familiar form of **Eugenio**

— ❦ —

Gerardo
Germanic — *ger* (spear) + *hard* (hard, brave)

— ❧ —

Germán
Germanic — *heri* meaning 'army' (implying 'soldier')

— ❧ —

Gervasio
Germanic — *ger* (spear) + *vass* (servant)

— ❧ —

Gilberto
Germanic — *gisil* (pledge) + *beraht* (bright)

— ❧ —

Gonzalo
A name of Germanic origin meaning 'warrior ready for battle'
Familiar form: Gonsito

— ❧ —

Gregorio
Greek — *gregorein* meaning 'to be vigilant, watchful'
Familiar form: **Orio**

— ❧ —

Guido
Germanic — *wit* meaning 'wide'

— ❧ —

Guillermo

Germanic — *wilja* (desire, hope) + *helm* (helmet, protection)
Guillermo Vilas (born 1952), Argentinian tennis player
Familiar forms: Guille, Guillo, Guillér
William is the English form

— ❦ —

Gustavo

Germanic — *gustav* meaning 'prosperous'
Familiar form: Gusty

— ❦ —

H

Héctor
Greek — *ehktor* meaning 'holding fast'
— ❦ —

Heriberto
Germanic — *here* (army) + *beraht* (bright)
— ❦ —

Hernán
Older form of **Fernando**
Hernán Cortés (1485-1547), Spanish conquistador
— ❦ —

Hilario
Latin — *hilaris* meaning 'cheerful'
— ❦ —

Hipolito
Greek — *hippos* (horse) + *lyein* (to free)
— ❦ —

Homero
Greek — *homerus* meaning 'hostage'
— ❦ —

Horacio
Latin — from *Horatius*, an old Roman family name
of obscure origin
— ❦ —

Hugo
Germanic — *hugh* meaning 'intelligence'

I

Ignacio
Latin — from *Egnatius*, an old Roman family name of obscure origin,
later identified with the Latin *ignis* meaning 'fire'
San Ignacio de Loyola (1491-1556), Spanish priest and
founder of the Society of Jesus (the Jesuits)
Basque forms: **Iñaki, Iñigo, Ñaki**
Familiar form: **Nacho**
Ignatius is the English form

Imanol
Basque form of **Manuel**

Indalecio
A name of Basque origin meaning 'strength'

Inocencio
Latin — *innocens* meaning 'innocent'

Iñaki
Basque form of **Ignacio**

— ❦ —

Íñigo
Basque form of **Ignacio**

— ❧ —

Isaac
Hebrew — *yishaq* meaning 'he laughs'
Isaac Albéniz (1867-1916), Spanish composer

— ❧ —

Isidoro
Greek — *Isis* (the Greek goddess of fertility) + *doron* (gift)
Alternative form: **Isidro**

— ❧ —

Isidro
Form of **Isidoro**
San Isidro is the patron saint of Madrid, the Spanish capital

— ❧ —

Ismael
Hebrew — *yishmael* meaning 'God hears'

— ❧ —

Israel
Hebrew — *yisrael* meaning 'he who struggles with God'

— ❧ —

Ito
Familiar form of **Arturo**

— ❧ —

J

Jacinto
Greek — *hyakinthos* meaning 'hyacinth'

— ❦ —

Jaime
Hebrew — *yaaqob* meaning 'supplanter'
Familiar forms: **Diego**, Jaimito
James is the English form

— ❦ —

Jandro
Familiar form of **Alejandro**

— ❦ —

Javier
Basque — *etxe-berri* meaning 'new house'
San Francisco Javier (St. Francis Xavier)(1506-1552),
a Spanish missionary priest, helped San Ignacio de Loyola
found the Jesuit order
Familiar form: Javi

— ❦ —

Jerónimo
Greek — *hieros* (holy) + *onyma* (name)

— ❦ —

Jesús
Hebrew — *yehoshua* meaning 'God saves'
Jesús Soto (born 1923), Venezuelan artist
Jesús is often combined with **María** to give **María Jesús**
Familiar forms: Chucho, Chus

— ☙ —

Joaquín
Hebrew — *yehoyakim* meaning 'God constructs'
Joaquín Rodrigo (born 1901), Spanish guitarist

— ☙ —

Jorge
Greek — *georgos* meaning 'farm worker'
Jorge Luis Borges (1899-1986), Argentinian writer
George is the English form

— ☙ —

José
Hebrew — *yosef* meaning 'He shall add (another son)'
José Ortega y Gasset (1883-1955), Spanish philosopher
José Carreras (1946), Spanish operatic tenor
José Clemente Orozco (1883-1949), Mexican artist and muralist
Pepe is a familiar form, the origin of which becomes clearer when
compared with *Giuseppe*, the Italian equivalent of **José**,
whose familiar form is *Zeppo*
Other familiar forms: Pepín, Pepito, **Pepe**
Joseph is the English form

~

José is often combined with other names, for example:
José Luis
José María

— ☙ —

Juan

Hebrew — *Yohanan* meaning 'God has been gracious'
Juan Carlos I (born 1938), King of Spain
Familiar forms: Juancito, Juanito
John is the English form

~

Juan is often combined with other names, for example:
Juan Antonio
Juan Carlos
Juan Luis
Juan Manuel
Juan María

— ❧ —

Julián

Form of **Julio**

— ❧ —

Julio

Latin — from *Julius*, an old Roman family name of obscure origin
Julio Iglesias (born 1943), Spanish singer
Alternative form: **Julián**

— ❧ —

Justino

Latin — *justus* meaning 'just, with integrity'
Alternative form: **Justo**

— ❧ —

Justo

Form of **Justino**

— ❧ —

K

Koldo
Basque form of **Luis**

Ladislao
Slavonic — *volod* (rule) + *slav* (glory)

— ❧ —

Lalo
Familiar form of **Eduardo**

— ❧ —

Laureano
Latin — *laureatus* meaning 'crowned with laurel'

— ❧ —

Lautaro
A name of Arabic origin meaning 'swift bird'

— ❧ —

Lázaro
Hebrew — *elazar* meaning 'God helps'
Lázaro Cárdenas (1895-1970), President of Mexico (1934-1940)

— ❧ —

Leandro
Greek — *leon* (lion) + *andros* (man)

— ❧ —

León
Latin — *leo* meaning 'lion'

— ❧ —

Leonardo
Germanic — *levon* (lion) + *hart* (strong)

— ❧ —

Leopoldo
Germanic — *liut* (people) + *balt* (brave)

— ❧ —

Liberto
Latin — *liberatus* meaning 'freed (slave)'

— ❧ —

Lisandro
Greek — *lysis* (freeing) + *andros* (man)

— ❧ —

Lito
Familiar form of **Cristóbal**

— ❧ —

Lope
Latin — *lupus* meaning 'wolf'

— ❧ —

Lorenzo
Latin — *laurus* meaning 'laurel'

— ❧ —

Luis

Germanic — *hluda* (famous) + *wiga* (war)
Luis Buñuel (1900-1983), Spanish film director
Basque form: **Koldo**
Familiar form: Lucho

~

Luis is often combined with other names, for example:
Luis Alberto
Luis Manuel
Luis María
Luis Miguel

— ❧ —

M

Macario
Greek — *makaros* meaning 'blessed'

— ❦ —

Manuel
Hebrew — *immanuel* meaning 'God is with us'
Manuel de Falla (1876-1946), Spanish composer
Manuel 'Manolo' Santana (born 1938), Spanish tennis player
Basque form: **Imanol**
Familiar forms: Manolo, Manolete, Nelo

— ❦ —

Marcelo
Form of **Marco**

— ❦ —

Marco
Latin — from *Marcus*, an old Roman family name probably derived
from *Mars*, the Roman god of war
Alternative forms: **Marcelo, Marcos**

— ❦ —

Marcos
Form of **Marco**

— ❦ —

María

See Girls' Names

Although **María** is a popular Spanish girl's name, it is often combined with boys' names, for example:

Ángel María

Antonio María

Carlos María

José María

Luis María

— ❧ —

Martín

Latin — *martinus* from *Mars*, the Roman god of war

Martín Tovar y Tovar (1827-1902), Venezuelan painter

Familiar form: Marty

— ❧ —

Mateo

Greek — *mattathiah* meaning 'gift of God'

Mateo Alemán (1547-1614), Spanish novelist and major literary figure

Alternative form: Matías

— ❧ —

Matías

Form of **Mateo**

— ❧ —

Mauricio

Latin — *maurus* meaning 'Moor' and therefore 'dark'

Alternative form: **Mauro**

— ❧ —

Mauro
Form of **Mauricio**

— ❧ —

Maximiliano
Latin — *maximus* (greatest) + *aemulus* (to equal)

— ❧ —

Máximo
Latin — *maximus* meaning 'greatest'

— ❧ —

Miguel
Hebrew — *mikhael* meaning 'Who is like God?'
Miguel de Cervantes (1547-1616), Spanish novelist, playwright,
poet and author of *Don Quixote*, is regarded as the most
important figure in Spanish literature
Miguel is often combined with **Ángel** to give **Miguel Ángel**
Familiar form: Mikel, Miky
Michael is the English form

— ❧ —

Mingo
Familiar form of **Domingo**

— ❧ —

Mini
Familiar form of **Fermín**

— ❧ —

Modesto
Latin — *modestus* meaning 'modest'

— ❦ —

Nacho
Familiar form of **Ignacio**

— ❦ —

Ñaki
Basque form of **Ignacio**

— ❦ —

Nando
Familiar form of **Fernando**

— ❦ —

Napoleón
Greek — *neapolis* (new city) + *leon* (lion)

— ❦ —

Nardo
Familiar form of **Bernardo**

— ❦ —

Nesti
Familiar form of **Ernesto**

— ❦ —

Nicanor
Greek — *nikaner* meaning 'victorious man'

— ❦ —

Nicasio
Greek — *nikasios* meaning 'victorious'

— ❦ —

Nicolás
Greek — *nike* (victory) + *laos* (people) meaning 'people's victory'
Nike was the winged goddess of victory in Greek mythology
Familiar form: Nico

— ❦ —

Nicomedes
Greek — *nike* (victory) + *medesthai* (to ponder)

— ❦ —

Nito
Familiar form of **Benito**

— ❦ —

O

Octavio
Latin — *octavus* meaning 'eighth'
Octavio Paz (born 1914), Mexican writer

Onofre
A name of Egyptian origin meaning 'one who unlocks goodness'

Orio
Familiar form of **Gregorio**

— ❦ —

Osvaldo
Germanic — *os* (god) + *weald* (power)

— ❦ —

P

Pablo
Latin — *paulus* meaning 'small'
Pablo Picasso (1881-1973), Spanish painter
Pablo Neruda (1904-1973), Chilean poet, Nobel Prize winner
Alternative form: **Paulo**
Familiar forms: Pedrín, Pedrucho, Pedruco
Paul is the English form

— ❦ —

Paco
Familiar form of **Francisco**
Paco de Lucía (born 1947), Spanish Flamenco guitarist

— ❦ —

Pancho
Familiar form of **Francisco**
Francisco 'Pancho' Villa (1878-1923), Mexican revolutionary leader

— ❦ —

Paquirrín
Familiar form of **Francisco**

— ❦ —

Pascual
Latin — *paschalis* meaning 'of Easter'

— ❦ —

Patrocinio
Latin — *patricius* meaning 'noble'

— ❦ —

Paulo
Form of **Pablo**

— ❦ —

Pedro
Greek — *petros* meaning 'rock, stone'
Pedro Almodóvar (born 1951), Spanish film producer and director
Peter is the English form

— ❦ —

Pepe
Familiar form of **José**

— ❦ —

Petronio
Latin — from *Petronius*, an old Roman family name taken from the
Greek *petros* meaning 'rock, stone'

— ❦ —

Plácido
Latin — *placidus* meaning 'placid, calm, tranquil'
Plácido Domingo (born 1941), Spanish operatic tenor

— ❦ —

Primo
Latin — *primus* meaning 'first'

— ❦ —

Procopio
Greek — *pro* (before) + *kopios* (copious, abundant)

— ❦ —

Próspero
Latin — *prosperus* meaning 'prosperous, successful'

— ❦ —

Prudencio
Latin — *prudens* meaning 'foreseeing, wise'

— ❦ —

𝒬

Quintín
Latin — *quintin* meaning 'fifth'
Alternative form: **Quinto**

— 🐝 —

Quinto
Form of **Quintín**

— 🐝 —

Quique
Familiar form of **Enrique**

— 🐝 —

Rafael
Hebrew — *rafael* meaning 'God has cured'
Familiar forms: Rafa, Rafi, Fafa
— ❦ —

Raimundo
Germanic — *ragin* (wise) + *mund* (protector)
— ❦ —

Ramiro
Germanic — *rad* meaning 'illustrious advice'
— ❦ —

Ramón
Germanic — *ragin* (wise) + *mund* (protector)
Familiar form: Moncho
— ❦ —

Raúl
Germanic — *rad* (counsel) + *wulf* (wolf)
Raúl Julia (1940-1994), Puerto Rican actor
— ❦ —

Reinaldo
Germanic — from *regen* and *weald* both meaning 'strength, power,'
the name implies 'great warrior'
— ❦ —

Renato
Latin — *renatus* meaning 'born again'
— ❧ —

Reubén
Hebrew — *reuben* meaning 'behold, a son!'
Alternative spelling: **Rubén**
Rubén Blades (born 1948), Panamanian-born salsa singer
— ❧ —

Ricardo
Germanic — *richi* (powerful) + *hard* (brave, hardy, strong)
Familiar forms: Rico, Ricky
Richard is the English form
— ❧ —

Rigoberto
Germanic — *rik* (ruler) + *beraht* (bright)
— ❧ —

Roberto
Germanic — *hrothi* (fame) + *beraht* (bright)
Familiar form: **Berto**
— ❧ —

Rodolfo
Germanic — *hruod* (fame) + *wulf* (wolf)
— ❧ —

Rodrigo
Germanic — *hruod* (fame) + *rik* (ruler)
— ❧ —

Rolando

Germanic — *hruod* (fame) + *land* (land)

S

Salomón
Hebrew — *shalom* meaning 'peace'

— ❦ —

Salvador
Spanish — *salvador* meaning 'savior, deliverer'
Salvador Allende (1908-1973), Chilean statesman and
President of Chile (1970-1973)
Salvador Dalí (1904-1989), Spanish surrealist painter
Familiar form: Salvi

— ❦ —

Samuel
Hebrew — *shama* meaning 'hear,' implying 'heard by God'

— ❦ —

Sancho
Latin — *sanctius* meaning 'sacred'

— ❦ —

Santiago
Spanish compound name — *san* (saint) + *Diego* (James)
Familiar form: **Yago**

— ❦ —

Saúl
Hebrew — *shaul* meaning 'asked for, borrowed'

— ❦ —

Sebastián
Latin — *sebastianus* meaning 'man from Sebasta,' a town in
Asia Minor

— ❦ —

Sergio
Latin — from *Sergius*, an old Roman family name of obscure origin

— ❦ —

Severiano
Latin — *severus* meaning 'severe, stern'
Alternative forms: Severino, Severo
Familiar forms: Seve, **Sevvy**

— ❦ —

Sevvy
Familiar form of **Severiano**
Sevvy Ballesteros (born 1957), Spanish golfer

— ❦ —

𝒯

Tadeo
Hebrew — biblical name of obscure origin
— ❧ —

Tebe
Familiar form of **Esteban**
— ❧ —

Teodoro
Greek — *theos* (God) + *doron* (gift)
— ❧ —

Teófilo
Greek — *theos* (God) + *philos* (loving)
— ❧ —

Timoteo
Greek — *time* (honor, respect) + *theos* (God)
— ❧ —

Tino
Familiar form of **Agustín**
— ❧ —

Tito
Possibly Greek — *tio* meaning 'to honor'
Tito Puente (born 1923), salsa band leader of Puerto Rican descent
— ❧ —

Tomás
Aramaic — *t'ome* meaning 'twin'

— —

Tonio
Familiar form of **Antonio**

— —

Toribio
Latin — of obscure origin

— —

Turo
Familiar form of **Arturo**

— —

U

Ulises
Latin — *Ulysses* after *Odysseus*, the Greek hero of
Homer's *Odyssey*

— ❦ —

Urbano
Latin — *urbano* meaning 'city dweller'

— ❦ —

𝒱

Valentín
Latin — *valere* meaning 'to be strong'

— ❦ —

Valeriano
Latin — *valere* meaning 'to be strong'
Alternative form: **Valerio**

— ❦ —

Valerio
Form of **Valeriano**

— ❦ —

Venturio
Latin — *ventura* meaning 'good fortune'
Alternative form: **Venturo**

— ❦ —

Venturo
Form of **Venturio**

— ❦ —

Vicente
Latin — *vincere* meaning 'to conquer'

— ❦ —

Vidal
Latin — *vitalis* meaning 'lively, full of life'

— ❧ —

Virgilio
Latin — after *Virgil*, the great Roman poet

— ❧ —

γ

Yago
Familiar form of **Santiago**

Z

Zacarías
Hebrew — *zechariah* meaning 'God has remembered'

— ❦ —

Zenobio
Greek — *zen* (of Zeus) + *bios* (life)

— ❦ —

Other Spanish-interest titles from Hippocrene Books...

Dictionaries and Language Guides

Children's Illustrated Spanish Dictionary
94 pages • 8 x 11 • 500 words with full color illustrations • 0-7818-0733-6 • W • $14.95hc • (206)

Spanish-English/English-Spanish Concise Dictionary (Latin American)
500 pages • 4 x 6 • 8,000 entries • 0-7818-0261-X • W • $11.95pb • (258)

Spanish-English/English-Spanish Compact Dictionary (Latin American)
310 pages • 3 x 4 • 8,000 entries • 0-7818-0497-3 • W • $8.95pb • (549)

Spanish-English/English-Spanish Dictionary and Phrasebook (Latin American)
220 pages • 3½ x 7 • 2,000 entries • 0-7818-0773-5 • W • $11.95pb • (261)

Spanish-English/English-Spanish Dictionary of Computer Terms
120 pages • 5 x 8 • 5,700 entries • 0-7818-0148-6 • W • $16.95hc • (36)

Spanish-English/English-Spanish Practical Dictionary
338 pages • 5 x 8 • 35,000 entries • 0-7818-0179-6 • NA • $9.95pb • (211)

Spanish Handy Dictionary
120 pages • 5 x 7 • 3,800 entries • 0-7818-0012-9 • W • $8.95pb • (189)

Spanish Grammar
224 pages • 5 x 8 • 0-87052-893-9 • W • $12.95pb • (273)

Spanish Verbs: Ser and Estar
220 pages • 5 x 8 • 0-7818-0024-2 • W • $8.95pb • (292)

Mastering Spanish
338 pages • 5 x 8 • 0-87052-059-8 • USA • $11.95pb • (527)
2 Cassettes: ca. 2 hours • 0-87052-067-9 • USA • $12.95 • (528)

Mastering Advanced Spanish
326 pages • 5 x 8 • 0-7818-0081-1 • W • $14.95pb • (413)
2 Cassettes: ca. 2 hours • 0-7818-0089-7 • W • $12.95 • (426)

Spanish Proverbs, Idioms and Slang
350 pages • 6 x 9 • 0-7818-0675-5 • W • $14.95pb • (760)

Dictionary of 1000 Spanish Proverbs
131 pages • 5½ x 8½ • 0-7818-0412-4 • W • $11.95pb • (254)

History

Mexico: An Illustrated History
150 pages • 5 x 7 • 50 illustrations • 0-7818-0690-9 • W • $11.95pb • (585)

Bilingual Poetry

Treasury of Spanish Love Poems, Quotations and Proverbs: Bilingual
128 pages • 5 x 7 • 0-7818-0358-6 • $11.95 • (589)
2 Cassettes: ca. 2 hours • 0-7818-0365-9 • $12.95 • (584)

Treasury of Spanish Love Short Stories in Spanish and English
157 pages • 5 x 7 • 0-7818-0298-9 • $11.95 • (604)

Folk Tales

Folk Tales from Chile
121 pages • 5 x 8 • 15 illustrations • 0-7818-0712-3 • W • $12.50hc • (78!

Cookbooks

Old Havana Cookbook (Bilingual)
Cuban Recipes in Spanish and English
128 pages • 5 x 7 • illustrations • 0-7818-0767-0 • W • $11.95hc • (590)

A Spanish Family Cookbook, Revised Edition
244 pages • 5 x 8 • 0-7818-0546-5 • W • $11.95pb • (642)

Prices subject to change without prior notice.
To order Hippocrene Books, contact your local bookstore, call (718) 454-2366, or write to: HIPPOCRENE BOOKS, 171 Madison Avenue, New York, NY 10016. Please enclose check or money order, adding $5.00 shipping (UPS) for the first book and $.50 for each additional title.